Poems

By the Shadowed Feather

Ulundi Jansen

www.trafford.com
North America & international
toll-free: 1 888 232 4444 (USA & Canada)
fax: 812 355 4082

Contents

Dedication

A Double Rainbow.
Linda, Izzi, Iman.
You saw my words and gave them wings.
I love you.

-Ulundi

Acknowledgements

Lisa my English teacher.
Friends and family for support in difficult times.

The Beginning

When I lost
everything
I found you.
A song, a book
and pen
that was new.
From a wing
that was broken
a feather survived,
in the shadow
it casted, words
came alive.
Give me stones
and journals
music and trees.
Bend and you'll
find
my words
at your feet.

Realisation

I need to pierce
that note of sigh
upon your chest
and draw a tear
of bloodstained quilt.
To hear the whisper
from your breath
confess!!
The splitting second
that you chose,
to while my heart
unguard with pain,
you stole my peace
you broke my chain.

Wonderland

I'm lost
between fairytales
somehow, they won't
let me go.
and even the silence
cannot tell me why.
How your hands always
seem to have
just the right touch.
Taking their time
till I am mine no more.
Leaving no inch of me
unmarked.
and when you breathe
so softly
I can feel the things
you dream
but sometimes
I slip to Wonderland
and I don't know
what it means.

Unwilling Prayer

Change for me
the face of hope,
that warms my
winter heart.
Turn the sun
halfway around
another soul of light
be found.
Erase the smile
of light I know
and paint a picture
real as snow.
All this I ask
unwillingly,
If You can
do this all
for me?

Divide

And I have torn
the page
where I wrote
that I will love you
forever.
For you
intruded my soul,
captured my
heart.
And as you turn
to go
I am left with halves
that was my
wholeness once.
Not as if
I didn't sense
your cruelness,
but I believed
that you would stay
for me.

Ties that bind

Beyond ties
of shamefully
hideaways,
memories crept
into my mind.
Like shadows
of a long lost bond
we shared.
And that far familiar
warmth
encircles my heart.
Don ever let me
lose you again.

Disillusionment

Everything
seemed
better.
Even reality
with a touch
of perfection.
But it was still
the same air,
and we all
breathed
still the same
sky
and we all
lived.
Still the rain
pours
and we all fall.
Here
and there,
everywhere.
So tell me again
when the sun
belonged
to you?

Escape

For a while
I was barefoot,
carefully testing
your soothing stream.
The turn in the road
closer
than I saw in my dream.
How dense this wood
carpets of leaves
small streaks
of sunlight
my sadness at ease.
Still standing tall
Cedars and Oaks
branches cast shadows
in silence
they spoke.
Dance with the moon
hide from the sun
as barefoot and willing
I'm starting
to run.

Silent words

But the only words
I know
are the ones
that is silent
and they're born
where fields lay still.
Sleep within the roots
of trees
and breathe soundless
like falling leaves.
And silent words
still mean the same
when written down
it spells your name.

Where you are

I've searched
the skies
uncovered clouds
faced the sun
with weakened eyes,
bribed the moon
asked for grace
and time cuts lines
across my face.
My mind, my soul,
between the two
within my heart
there I found you.

Healing

This is my world
living on the inside
and the silence
still clings
to my bones.
But we collided
and you filled
my wounds
with words.
So when I leak
from heart
to hand
in my silence
understand
that now
you own
my hand.

Longing

I missed
your smile
today.
The way your demons
play across your eyes,
the move of your hands,
your laugh.
And I could almost feel
the pain
you left upon my skin.

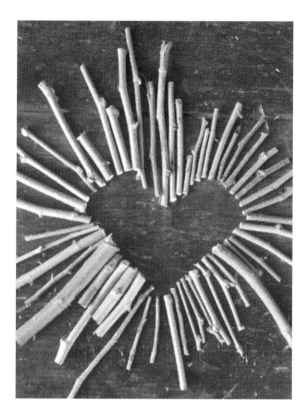

Riddle

Pick up sticks
lay them straight
count with me
almost eight....
When it's midnight,
I will know
moon will
change,
a fading glow.
But when the sun
announce the
day
I'll hear your voice
and we will play.

Always

And my heart
will always beat
for you.
Wild when you
touch me,
weak when you
miss me,
strong when you
hurt me.
And you should
always feel my heart
it beats within
yours.

Acceptance

And even if I search
for wrongs
in all of this,
and even if I page
through laws of mankind,
gods and hopeless
perfect beings,
still I feel no quilt
no shame.
Just truth
like roots of trees
that search for life
through sand and rock,
so will my soul
still search
for what it needs
in you.

Dreams

If you would steal
my dreams
beneath the shadows,
and be a fallen Saint
amongst the crowds,
then I will shout
my love by thunder
lay you down
in cotton clouds.
Fill your empty spaces
feed your darkest needs
Between the silent
shadows
my dreams are still
asleep.

Morning and night

When day is born
my thoughts awake
with you.
How softly
you sneak into
my day.
Then as darkness
falls upon my eyes
and sleep is hard
to find
you once again
remain to be
the last thought
of my mind.

Next time

Fragments
Partial
Pieces
There is no
completely.
So we live
half a tale
and I smile
at the moon.
Between pauses
till next time,
days are wasted
and I
will see you soon.

Denial

The mind is bleeding
the words at war
and silence keeps
screaming,
can't find the door.
A picture is scattered
by will, not by fate
but it's pieces
keep crawling
forever's to late.
Deny with the mind
what's true to the soul
let the heart be the
victim
and fear
have it all.

Journey

Time was endless
but not for her.
How she needed
the salt.
But the ocean
is to far
for such a short
journey.
So she stepped into
the river
that would flow into
the sea.
How thirsty one becomes
in such a long way
home.

Your Name

I hear your voice
like a midnight
poem
scrolling softly
through my mind.
Colour all my
daydreams
blind me with
that smile.
How can I
not miss you
the times that
we're apart.
Your name
is in my
pocket
on a folded
paper heart.

Halves

Half a moon
half of dawn
and twigs and trees
and night
Half of paper
half of white
and half of ink
that writes.
Half of grief
like make believe
and half of what
you feel
Half of light and sun
and shame
and partial scars
that heal.
Half the flight
of soaring birds
half the strength
of wind
Half your words
will reach my ear
and half I will not
hear.
Turn half my head
from facing you
say half the things
I feel.
Then halfway, when I'm
almost there,
completely I will share
and maybe then
for once for you
I can cry
half a tear.

Restore

In the sureness
of nothing
restore my soul.
Disguard these
make believes
and turn to dust
the road away
from home.
Let me hear
the song of wind
played by fingertips
of leaves.
Curve around my feet
the feel of soil.
Ground my wait
so I can dwell no more.
Let me sleep
in silence, wake me
by the breath of one
that holds my soul.
Paint it on my skin
to never
let it go.

Ulundi Jansen

Your Bonsai poem

Wee little fellows,
of no woods, or
streams or fields,
Shaped by the hands
of lovers,
of twigs and curves
and feel.
Bend by shapeless
wire
trimmed by means
of growth,
bleeding on the edges
where new leaves
can't wait
to show.
Sacred bark will cover
scars induced
by thee.
If we can tell
the story
of how wee came
to be,
It would be in
only one word
Wee are.. destiny.
** (wee : meaning small

Marked

You carved
your name
in the bark
of my heart.
The roots
of my soul
feels your warmth
where it's dark.
And when leaves
drip the wet
from the tears
of the rain,
My branches
will hold you
again and again.

Visions of you

Try so hard
to let it be
raise my eyes
above
in search
and plea
but everywhere
they dwell
still images
of you
and me.

Piano Poem

Do you know
the way your face
changes?
The way
your being shifts
the line of feel
from black and white
to fingertips, is bare,
an undeniable passage
of pure and uncontrolled
emotion,
forced to mark
each single line
that touch your face.
And I can stare
with eyes wide shut
and feel
each word you play.
A rage,
an unspoken urge,
like devastating
truths
that's known
by only
you.

Mom

They colour
the ocean,
your eyes
so blue.
When the wind
lifts me up
I know that it's
you.
The things
that we share
the pain
we went through
I needed an angel
and God gave me
YOU.

Search

Softest of
dark,
deepest of
night,
tracing fine lines
around shadows
and mark,
spaces between
nothing that
moves
leaving a trail
as I'm searching
for you.

Retreat

Remove so softly
these prints
of feel
from out my heart,
as if never
I was drawn
into your field
of make believe
and chase no more
these fireflies
you pour
around my dark.

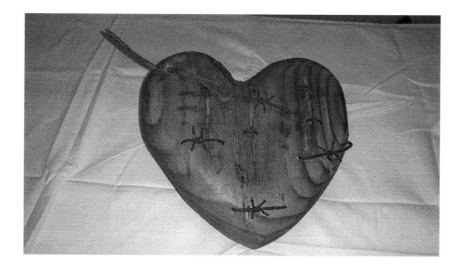

Be Still

When the silence
becomes peace,
the stillness
of my heart
a safe cage,
then once more
I find
solitude
in my unspokenness

End

I have seen
the end of it.
Ask, receive
regret retreat,
one step closer
in deceit.

Ripped the darkness
from these walls
where roots are claws
and silence calls.

Tear the covers
of each page
that hides the real,
the feel, the phrase
of each destructive
lifeless word
that's uttered, written
spoken, poured.
The salt the sweat
the heartless tides
of grief that sheds
a tear inside

Softly frown
upon the wait
a maybe someday
definate fate.

Song of love

The song of love
was never meant
for the secret, the
words of feel
not for the bold.
All else is sad,
like shadows and
the sudden glimpse
of real.
When our fields are
empty
we become hunters
of love, poems
and touch
as tender as the
the moon.
But for the wise,
to seal the pain
and bleed inside.

Rejection

Where did the time go
and the moments
that you could feel
my soul?
Rusted lie these words
here, the ones
that found your eyes
and tied my heart
to yours.
Unturned pages
craved by you
no more
I left it here
for you to find
so many times before.
No blame, just feel
the strangeness
of its hold.

Time

In silent sheets
of lines,
rest the unspoken.
How the chains
of rhymes
can scream
of truths unbroken.
Time will turn
the white sheet's colour,
ink that fades
change words
into another.
The verse the feel
the line
somehow still lives
within another
time.

Request

I want to be
the light behind
your eyes.
See that silent place
you go
when I can't find you.

I want to know
the rhythm
of your blood
when I can't
feel you.

I want to search
the corners
of your soul
so I can leave
before I lose you.

Sacrifice

Like headless statues
of granite souls
all images goes quite.
I placed the collage
of your face
on the altar
of broken dreams,
torn inside,
where ripped
from out my heart.
Recklessly i loved
with no shame or quilt.

Make me unafraid
of this pain,
i silently pray,
as want weaves through
my bones and keep
my constant hunger
alive, feeding
my brokenness
with flames of passion.

Burn to ashes
broken images of you.
As fallen angels
we have to
grow new wings
and fly.

My Heart

Where images breed
and all unwind
like shattered leaves
not to be found,
where thoughts of you
make reason hide
and steel my sleep,
My Mind my Mind.

The space unknown
that should be clear,
where peace should grow
untouched by fear,
the place you own
My Soul my Soul.

Where secrets sleep
and shadows thrive
where demons play
the place you hide,
where scars
stand guard
My Heart my Heart.

Hurt

Don't wait
I have uncovered all.
Don't you see?
My chest is naked,
clear and open,
still so full
within.
How this heavy
sadden ocean
longs to be
released.
I beg of you
in silence
one step closer
stab me deep.
I need that wounds
to leak this sore
and pounding waves inside.
Pooling slowly
round my feet
till i feel
clenched No more.

Hope

And softly night
will fall
upon the wishes
of us all.
The voice that speaks
from out my heart
went to sleep now
in the dark.
My face I turned
I saw afar
the birth of just
the perfect star.
So much stronger
by the wait
with bones of steel
will meet my fate.
The book will close
on you and me,
our story sealed
in memory.

Yo-Yo

In silence I speak
of the things I recall
covered by dust
seeming so small.
Awakened again
clenching my soul
the ebb and the flow
the yes and the no.
Nothing seems real
with the fall and the rise
of feelings that mimic
the way of the tides.
Why should I wait
on what's different today
on this game that I hate?
Will go outside
and play.

Play

Eyelids of sunshine
flicker through rays
fights with the coldness
for corners to play.
Winter came sudden
forming new art,
Craving and wanting
this thing called
my heart.

Fading

So tell me why
my words are few
and growing weak?
I can see the sun
is turning.
Change of season,
fading heart.
Hold on tighter
paper white
as breaking lead
release the night.

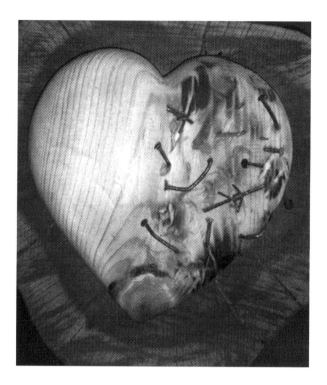

Different

Otherness
still stirring
where the wind
don't blow
and a pinch of
pain
lingers
just below.
But there's no point
in this and that
you know.
Just holding on
to when
to let it go.

Secrets

When you know
and it covers all
like the ocean,
leaving no space
in the corners
of you soul.
And you live
and you live,
untill your limbs
grow weak
Feel the
inbetween
moments,
and you still
don't speak.
Within each
waking hour
lies a truth so
rare
And you cling
to the feel
with a wide eyed
stare.

Hideaway

For these are
my moments
and mine alone.
in a place
i can't be found.
My maze of secrets
clear as light
where shadowed
feathers blind
your sight.
All my words
get lost in here,
still ink,
the silent stain
will keep on edging
endless tales
written
with no names.

Untold

So I write the story
from where I bleed.
There's no walls to
the space where
the hole runs deep.
All our lifetimes will
end,
by the flaws in the tale
still it grants me some
moments, with the feel
that prevails.
Between all the lines
lies the truth
as words meet
in the story
of my pain
the one you'll
never read.

Escape II

Take my hand
hold on tight
moon won't
be there
every night.
tear the pages
climb the wall
words on pages
seem so small
when the book
has closed
the day
half the moon
will fly away.

Stay

Do not fade
from me now.
You
made from dust
that lives with trees
and play the songs
of wind.
Stay
now that I am born
with new eyes
to see the light
in all my darkness.
Show me how
to play these shadows
and taste the salt
of uncried tears
no more.

The Edge

When their eyes
have no more
questions
for they look
within the soul
although the heart's
still beating,
broken, to be whole.
When breaths are
thin and shallow
and time has
no more pride
They don't see
what we fear for
because the eyes
don't say goodbye.

Touch

Coarse in feel
carving heart
precisely forming
pencil line art
only to be
understood
fine grooves
in weeping wood.

Smooth in trace
faceless page
curving words
ending phrase.
Ink it all
never tell
secrets deep
living hell.

Burn in touch
clench in red
shivering tears
truths unsaid
moist on petals
river deep
closing eyes
peaceful sleep
Night has fallen
shadows stand
staring at
an empty hand.

Silhouette

The silence still clings
to my bones
I have named you
in a whisper.
Painted you face
on the pages
of the clouds
And when the
mist of morning
lays your breath
upon my skin
I hold on
to your shadow
then return you
to the wind.

In Pain

Don't wait
I have uncovered all.
Don't you see?
My chest is naked,
clear and open, yet
so full within.
How this heavy sadden
ocean longs to be released.
And I'm waiting,
Beg in silence for you
to take one step closer.
Stab me deep
i need that wounds,
to leak this sore
and pounding waves
inside.
Pooling slowly round my feet
till i feel clenched
No more.

Close

Don't you know?
The phantom
in my dreams,
my soul has known
a lifetime,
drew lines across
the sky
and traced
the outlines
of your face.
Never have I been
so close
to almost
touch you.

Listen

I was not anger.
You could feel
my hurt, as if
it belongs to you.
Holding me
till it was empty
inside.
You know so well
the sound of my heart
when it becomes too small.
You keep it
moving.
You still linger
on the folds of my skin,
recklessly insane.
Turn me to water
every time you say
my name.

Knowing

It was rare
like a storybook story.
Not the fairytale ones,
I know now.
Those had happy endings.
But it's still my story
and in it,
I am the one
who dies,
inside.
Yet I cannot close
the book.
I'm still waiting
for you
to write
The END.

My love

And if I tell
where grace is found,
that silent place
that knows
my mind.

And if I say
where I go to
when all I need
is all of you.

And if I speak
of truths unknown
then it may turn
your heart
to stone.

And if I whisper
in the storm
of what has died
and what was born,
the moment that
she spoke to me
And if I tell
my love....

Feel

I recall nothing
as if born blind
There is no resemblance
to the feel of you
The way your heat crawls
down my skin, the burn
the sigh the weep.
And I am bound
to these secret
forbidden moments.
Returning to me once
and once again.

Awareness

The wind plays
lightly
through the trees
and with the stirring
of each leaf
I feel you
brush against my skin.

Withdrawn

I keep on holding you
for one and two and
many sleepless nights.
If I should close
my eyes,
the feel of you
would draw our lines,
a silhouette of shadows
sleeping tight.
It's crawling close the
end of us
our picture will remain,
when darkness comes
just look at it
I hear you say again,
we always were
a perfect fit don't
leave an empty space.
And I'll recall that moment
it was written on your face.

Mended

It was broken
but I saw a new day
a clear sky
a new night
a million stars
in your eyes.
Then dreams
closed my mind
sheltered my soul,
fear to steal my
sleep no more.
So when the white
of moon turns grey
I'll see you smile
and turn my way.

Shelter

In the branches
of my tree
I hold
a resting place
for you
and dancing flowers
for your smile.
My bark a shelter
for your fears.
I shed a thousand
leaves each day
to catch you
gently
as your hands will
open
and you let go.

Saying Goodbye

A mind so clear,
hands still strong
a few tender pictures
and a paperclip bond.
Binding together
years that's gone by,
tapping the notes
of a song in his mind.
At peace with a smile
for those who cry.
The strength of a cedar
made the small trees grow
Lights the fire in our hearts
that forever will glow.

Regret

Because they never
leave me
these words.
They became my breath,
my unspoken voice,
my secrets, my hope
my pain.
I found holy ground
once,
to lay them down
but they became
my shame.
The sun just shines
while the dry winds race,
blowing ashes of ink
all over my face.

You know

I first saw your eyes
and then your lips
as the whispered
"oh there you are"
And I said nothing.
By holding you
my heart spoke
a million tears
and you softly said
"I know"

Midnight

I skipped with you
past shadows
bounced from
leaf to leaf,
splashed your face
with dewdrops
put your fears
at ease.
How I love
these long nights
staring at the stars
feel the sense of
healing
as you touch
my scars.

Mute

I will love
in endless words
unspoken.
I won't cry
for tears
will steal the secrets
from my soul.
Within these walls
remains a single memory,
staring,
from my heart's
empty frame.
And as the darkness
fills each silent corner
I still can hear
the whisper of your
name.

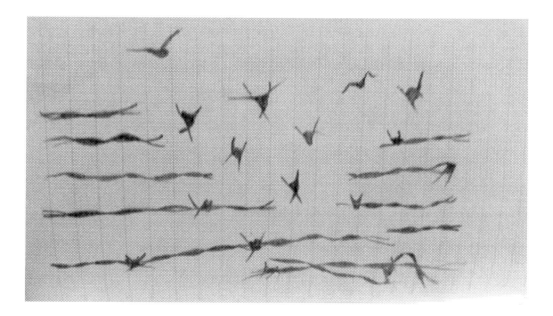

Wired

Tied too long
bound so strong
in tangled fates
of being
wrong.
Twisted points
sharpened edges
tightly bend
in safe protection.
So bright your light
encircled me
rusted hopes
to just break free.
Fly like ravens
to the sky
and for once
so free
am I.

Love

Then it fell
from my lips
the four letter word
and I broke my vow.
And now you fill
the corners
of my mind,
pace barefoot
in the chambers
of my heart,
give me songs
that make my soul
sing.
And so much space
is wasted
when I don't
feel you.

Seekers

Hush then, for the
tender has been taken.
The soft of heart and
dreamers of conformity.
Bound to peaceful nights
and following days.
Believers of contentment,
fulfilling make believes
in the quiet of everyday life.
Few were the ones,
left amongst the stretching
shadows of fierce growing trees
Driven by wild beating hearts,
craving fast breaths, pulsing
rhythm and endless passion.
Those were the ones,
who became,
restless, driven, prey.
Unbound, to be free
the ones that stayed
untouched.

Bound

Tie my hands
have thy way
for innocent
I stand.
How can I be put
to blame
with ropes
around my hands?
For its not me
I'm playing blind
I just
seduce you
with my mind.
And as I'm watching
playing you
from where I stand
the blame's
on you.

Go

The light in you
has died for me
I watch your
slow retreat.
Take it all,
cold defeat,
is what you left
for me.
Your always
I will never see
and never
won't remain.
I won't look back
to watch you leave
for now I'm free
Of pain.

Happy feet

Paint me picture
dance me a play
two sets of
of footprints
taken away.
Whenever you
wonder
go take a look
I once was a hero
in your
childhood
storybook.

Dad

At first
my feet got lost
in your footprints.
They were still small.
As they grew,
I sometimes wondered
of that darkness
you kept inside.
I used to wash my hands
just the way you did,
and you smiled.
The foam
on the hair of your arms
I dried so many times.

My feet found shape
in your footprints,
as I was your child,
saw you slaved
against your demons
as I played
not far behind.
How deep they carved
a trail, in between your eyes.

Still some time
to measure
almost a perfect fit,
and I can hide my broken
just the way
you did.